Mapping
OCEANS

Barbara Bakowski

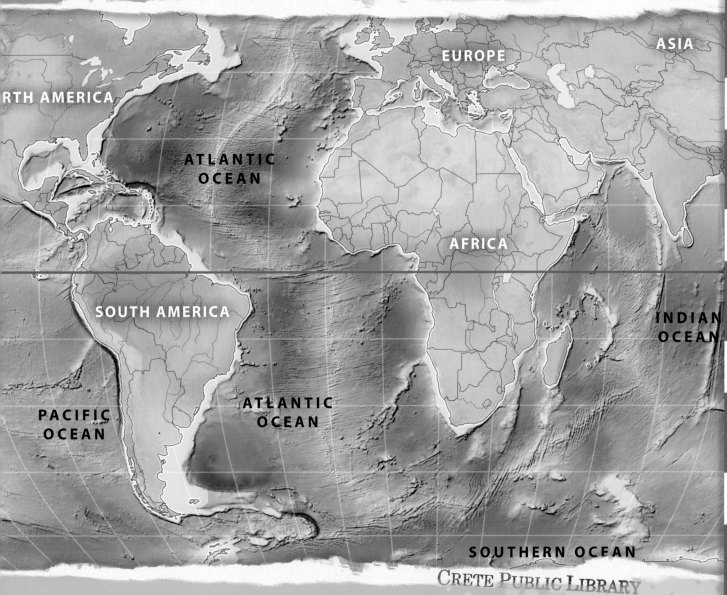

Marshall Cavendish
Benchmark
New York

This edition first published in 2011 in the United States
by Marshall Cavendish Benchmark.

Marshall Cavendish Benchmark
99 White Plains Road
Tarrytown, NY 10591
www.marshallcavendish.us

Copyright © 2011 Q2AMedia

Published by Marshall Cavendish Benchmark
An imprint of Marshall Cavendish Corporation

Other Marshall Cavendish Offices:
Marshall Cavendish International (Asia) Private Limited, 1 New Industrial Road, Singapore 536196 • Marshall Cavendish
International (Thailand) Co Ltd. 253 Asoke, 12th Flr, Sukhumvit 21 Road, Klongtoey Nua, Wattana, Bangkok 10110,
Thailand • Marshall Cavendish (Malaysia) Sdn Bhd, Times Subang, Lot 46, Subang Hi-Tech Industrial Park, Batu Tiga,
40000 Shah Alam, Selangor Darul Ehsan, Malaysia

Marshall Cavendish is a trademark of Times Publishing Limited

Library of Congress Cataloging-in-Publication Data
Bakowski, Barbara.
Mapping oceans.
p. cm.—(Mapping our world)
Includes bibliographical references and index.
Summary: "Introduces maps and teaches essential mapping skills, including how to create,
use, and interpret maps of oceans"—Provided by publisher.
ISBN 978-1-60870-117-9
1. Atlases. 2. Oceans. I. Title.
G1021.B2236 2011
526.09162—dc22
2010001563

Created by Q2AMedia
Series Editor: Deborah Rogus
Art Director: Harleen Mehta
Client Service Manager: Santosh Vasudevan
Project Manager: Kumar Kunal
Line Artist: Vinay Kumar
Coloring Artist: Subhash Vohra
Photo research: Ekta Sharma, Rajeev Parmar

The photographs in this book are used by permission and through the courtesy of:

Cover: NASA/Goddard Space Flight Center Scientific Visualization Studio
Half title: Joe LeMonnier

4: Jan Rysavy/Istockphoto; 5: Specta/Shutterstock; 6: Joe LeMonnier; 7t: Steve Estvanik/Shutterstock; 7b: Joe LeMonnier;
8-9: Joe LeMonnier; 10: Joe LeMonnier; 12: Bigstock; 13t: Emrahselamet/Shutterstock; 13b: Paul Clarke/Shutterstock;
15: NOAA; 17t: Joe LeMonnier; 19t: Joe LeMonnier; 20l: Tonylady/Shutterstock; 20r: Joe LeMonnier;
22l: John A. Anderson/Shutterstock; 22r: Harmonia/Dreamstime; 23: Ocean Image Photography/Shutterstock;
24: Shutterstock; 25t: Bettmann/Corbis; 25b: Fitor Angel M/Photolibrary; 26t: NASA; 26c: NASA; 26b: Jan Martin Will/
Shutterstock; 27: Florida Keys National Marine Sanctuary/NOAA; 28-29: Jarvis Gray/Shutterstock;
28: ESA; 29: George Burba/Shutterstock

Q2AMedia Art Bank: 6, 10, 11, 12, 13, 14, 15, 16, 17, 18, 19, 21, 22, 25, 27

Printed in Malaysia

1 3 5 6 4 2

Contents

Our Wet World 4

Reading Maps 6

Oceans of the World 8

Navigating the Oceans 10

Ocean in Motion 12

Deep, Deeper, Deepest 16

Ocean Treasures 20

Mapping the Future 24

Awesome Oceans 28

Glossary 30

To Learn More 31

Index 32

Words in **bold** are defined in the Glossary.

Our Wet World

When most people think of Earth, they think of land. But look at the map below. Most of our world is water!

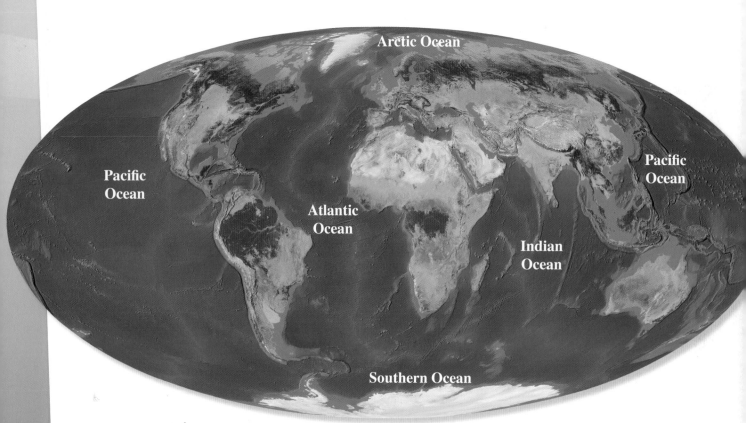

Arctic Ocean

Pacific Ocean

Pacific Ocean

Atlantic Ocean

Indian Ocean

Southern Ocean

Oceans Alive

Earth is the only planet known to have liquid water on its surface, which makes life on Earth possible. Almost all of this water is in the oceans—97 percent, in fact! Less than one percent of Earth's water is in lakes and rivers. This probably explains why, according to scientists, life started in the oceans. It also explains why we depend on the oceans for survival.

As this map shows, water covers about 70 percent of the planet. The ocean's surface area is larger than the surface area of all the continents combined!

Why Map the Oceans?

Oceans are the planet's largest habitat. They make up about 99 percent of the living space on Earth and are home to nearly half of all **species**. Earth's oceans serve many other functions, too. They play an important role in regulating the weather and climate. They supply us with food and minerals. They also provide an important means of transportation.

A coral reef is a fascinating ocean habitat. It is a warm, shallow-water neighborhood for thousands of colorful creatures. Fish, eels, and **sea anemones** are just a few of the creatures that can be found here.

Did You Know?
Most of the underwater world remains unexplored!

Reading Maps

Maps can provide information about all kinds of land and water features. For example, ocean maps can show **tides** or water temperatures. They can even show good areas for fishing!

Using Map Tools

Different types of maps are used for different purposes. Most maps, though, have certain elements, or tools, in common. By learning to use these tools, you can read almost any map.

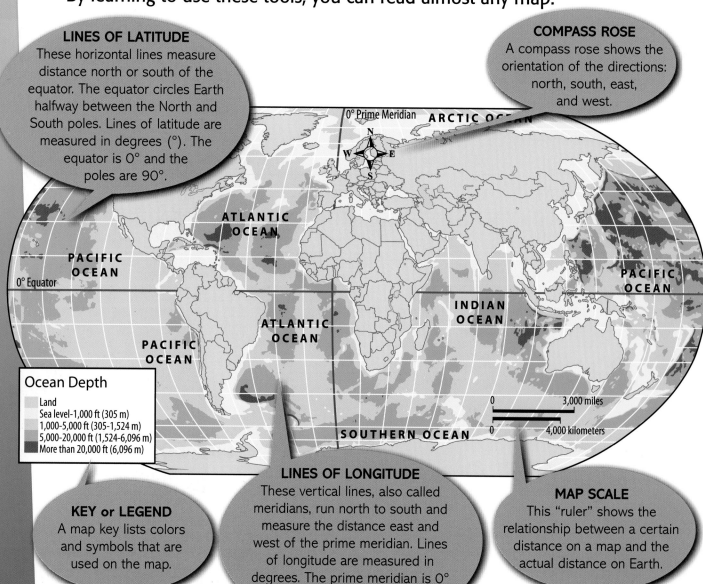

LINES OF LATITUDE
These horizontal lines measure distance north or south of the equator. The equator circles Earth halfway between the North and South poles. Lines of latitude are measured in degrees (°). The equator is 0° and the poles are 90°.

COMPASS ROSE
A compass rose shows the orientation of the directions: north, south, east, and west.

0° Prime Meridian ARCTIC OCEAN

N
W — E
S

ATLANTIC OCEAN

PACIFIC OCEAN

0° Equator

ATLANTIC OCEAN

INDIAN OCEAN

PACIFIC OCEAN

PACIFIC OCEAN

SOUTHERN OCEAN

Ocean Depth
- Land
- Sea level-1,000 ft (305 m)
- 1,000-5,000 ft (305-1,524 m)
- 5,000-20,000 ft (1,524-6,096 m)
- More than 20,000 ft (6,096 m)

0   3,000 miles
0   4,000 kilometers

KEY or LEGEND
A map key lists colors and symbols that are used on the map.

LINES OF LONGITUDE
These vertical lines, also called meridians, run north to south and measure the distance east and west of the prime meridian. Lines of longitude are measured in degrees. The prime meridian is 0° and meridians measure up to 180° east or west.

MAP SCALE
This "ruler" shows the relationship between a certain distance on a map and the actual distance on Earth.

What Maps Can We Use?

We can use several types of maps to study the oceans. To navigate, or travel from place to place, sea captains use nautical charts. Bathymetric maps are made by measuring the depth of the ocean. They show the ups and downs of the ocean bottom. Thematic maps display specific types of information, such as water temperatures or shipping routes.

Some of the most detailed maps are made using new technology. Scientists use special **satellites** and **radar** to take measurements and pictures of the ocean. They use this data to create topographic maps that show differences in sea surface height. Scientists also create maps that show the speed, energy, and direction of ocean **currents**.

Adding an Ocean

In 2000 the International Hydrographic Organization set new ocean boundaries, creating the Southern (Antarctic) Ocean. Once part of the southern Atlantic, Indian, and Pacific oceans, the world's newest ocean extends from the coast of Antarctica up to 60° south latitude.

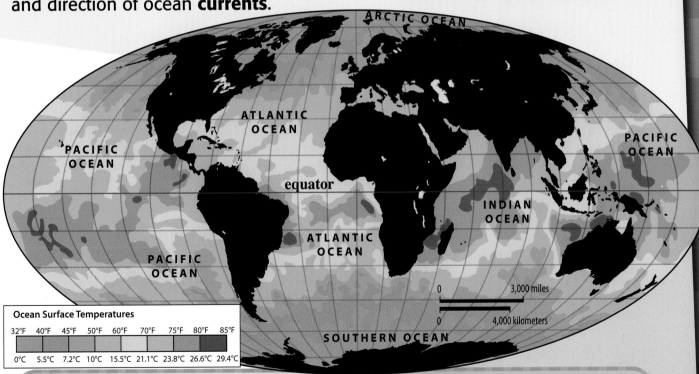

ARCTIC OCEAN

ATLANTIC OCEAN

PACIFIC OCEAN

PACIFIC OCEAN

equator

INDIAN OCEAN

ATLANTIC OCEAN

PACIFIC OCEAN

SOUTHERN OCEAN

| 0 | | | | | 3,000 miles |
| 0 | | | | | 4,000 kilometers |

Ocean Surface Temperatures

32°F	40°F	45°F	50°F	60°F	70°F	75°F	80°F	85°F
0°C	5.5°C	7.2°C	10°C	15.5°C	21.1°C	23.8°C	26.6°C	29.4°C

Map It! In Hot Water

This thematic map uses color to show the ocean's surface temperature.

Read It!

Use the key to read the map. Where is the water warmest? The coldest?

Oceans of the World

Look at any map of the world. The oceans are actually one huge body of water! The ocean names and boundaries were decided over time for historical, cultural, political, and scientific reasons.

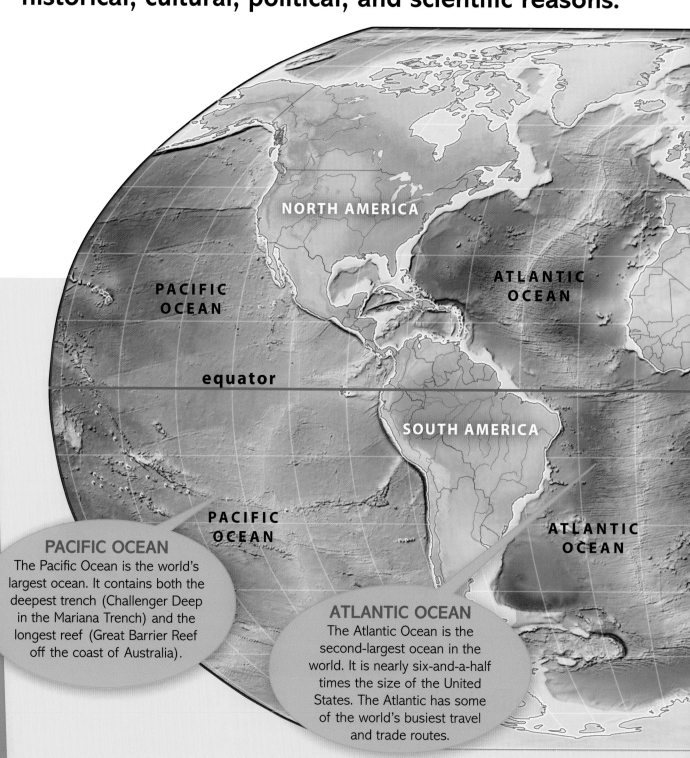

NORTH AMERICA

ATLANTIC OCEAN

PACIFIC OCEAN

equator

SOUTH AMERICA

PACIFIC OCEAN

ATLANTIC OCEAN

PACIFIC OCEAN
The Pacific Ocean is the world's largest ocean. It contains both the deepest trench (Challenger Deep in the Mariana Trench) and the longest reef (Great Barrier Reef off the coast of Australia).

ATLANTIC OCEAN
The Atlantic Ocean is the second-largest ocean in the world. It is nearly six-and-a-half times the size of the United States. The Atlantic has some of the world's busiest travel and trade routes.

Water, Water Everywhere

The world has five oceans: the Atlantic, Pacific, Indian, Arctic, and Southern (or Antarctic) oceans. There are also smaller bodies of water called seas. Seas are usually connected to oceans by **channels** of water.

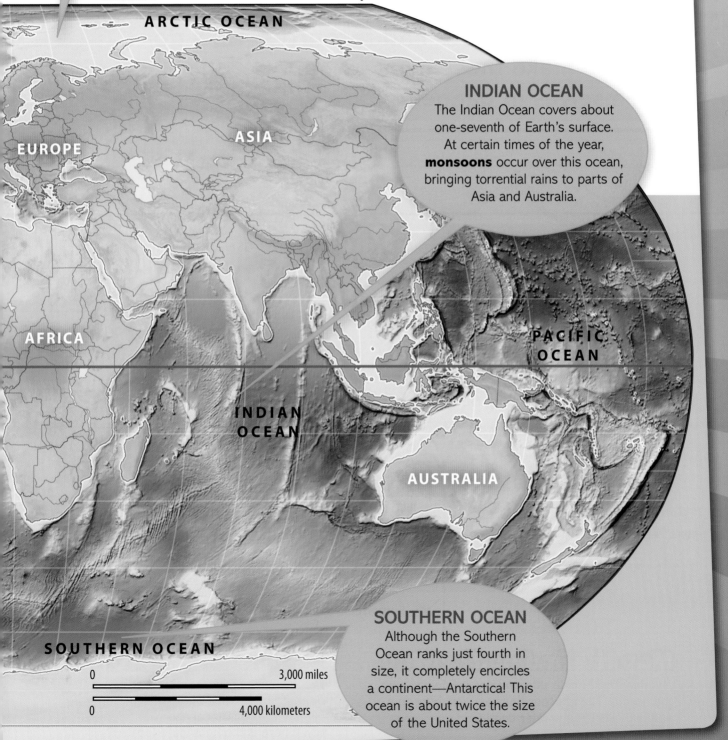

ARCTIC OCEAN
The Arctic Ocean is the smallest ocean. Much of its surface is covered with ice that is about 10 feet (3 meters) thick. The Arctic is home to **endangered** walruses and whales.

INDIAN OCEAN
The Indian Ocean covers about one-seventh of Earth's surface. At certain times of the year, **monsoons** occur over this ocean, bringing torrential rains to parts of Asia and Australia.

SOUTHERN OCEAN
Although the Southern Ocean ranks just fourth in size, it completely encircles a continent—Antarctica! This ocean is about twice the size of the United States.

ARCTIC OCEAN

EUROPE

ASIA

AFRICA

PACIFIC OCEAN

INDIAN OCEAN

AUSTRALIA

SOUTHERN OCEAN

0   3,000 miles

0   4,000 kilometers

Navigating the Oceans

We travel across oceans for many reasons: to go on journeys, to ship goods, to protect our country, and to find resources. How do people make these trips without putting themselves in danger?

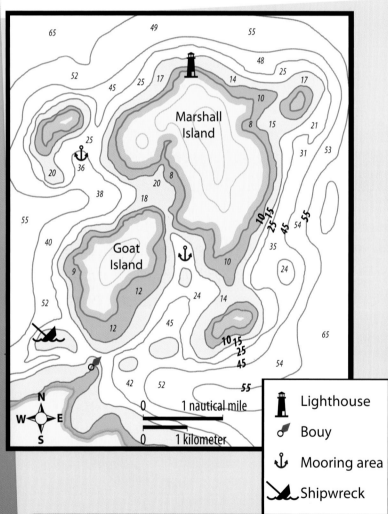

65 49 55
52 17 48 25
45 25 25 14 17
52 10
Marshall Island 8 15 21
25 31 53
20 36 8
38 20
18
55
40 35
Goat Island 10 24
9 12
52 24 14
45
12 65
42 52 54
0   1 nautical mile
0   1 kilometer

N W E S

🗼 Lighthouse
⚓ Bouy
⚓ Mooring area
🚢 Shipwreck

Getting From Here to There

People use maps called nautical charts to navigate oceans safely. These charts identify locations and show the distances between them. They also indicate water depth and include information about hazards, tides, and currents.

Recreational boaters use nautical charts to sail safely. People who fish look at nautical charts to locate fishing grounds. Commercial shippers rely on charts to plan the shortest, safest, and most economical routes. Nautical charts can even help people locate sunken treasure!

Map It! Finding the Way

Nautical charts help ship captains safely navigate the oceans. The **contour lines** and numbers on a nautical chart show water depth.

Read It!

The numbers on this nautical chart give the water depth in feet. Blue areas indicate shallow water. Look at the symbols in the key. Where is the lighthouse located?

Activity

Materials
- tracing paper
- colored pencils

Ahoy, Captain!

How do captains use nautical charts to plan a safe route? Follow these steps to find out.

1. Use tracing paper and a pencil to trace the nautical chart on page 10. Color the land brown. Color the water different shades of blue or leave it white, depending on the depth.

2. Draw the symbols (buoy, mooring area, lighthouse, and shipwreck) in the correct positions.

3. Use the depth numbers on the chart to map a safe course from the lighthouse to Goat Island. *Caution:* Avoid obstacles and water that is less than 20 feet deep.

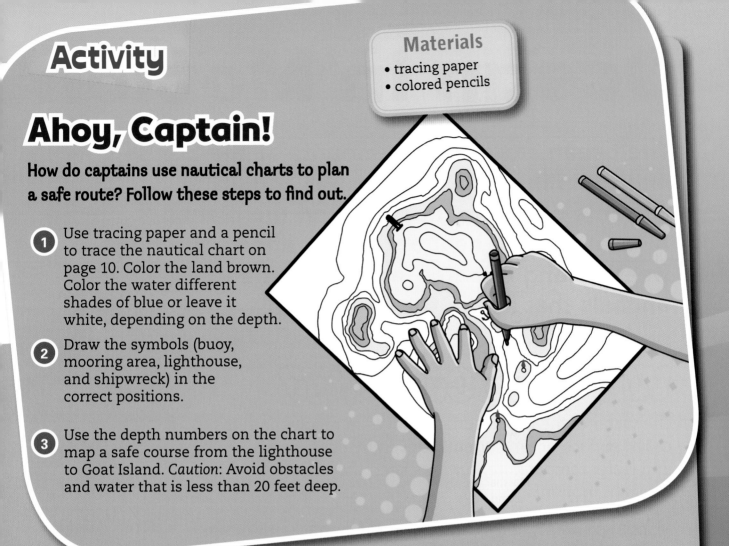

Goods Over Water

Cargo ships, barges, and tankers carry the things people need all over the world. In fact, nearly 90 percent of all traded goods travels by ship! To make sure everything arrives safe and sound, shipping companies use maps to plan their routes.

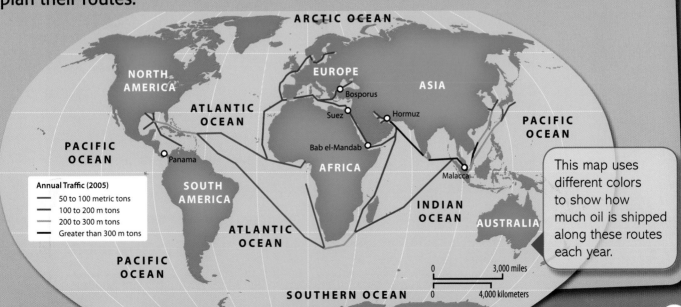

ARCTIC OCEAN

NORTH AMERICA

EUROPE

ASIA

Bosporus

ATLANTIC OCEAN

Suez

Hormuz

PACIFIC OCEAN

PACIFIC OCEAN

Panama

Bab el-Mandab

AFRICA

Malacca

SOUTH AMERICA

INDIAN OCEAN

AUSTRALIA

Annual Traffic (2005)
— 50 to 100 metric tons
— 100 to 200 m tons
— 200 to 300 m tons
— Greater than 300 m tons

ATLANTIC OCEAN

PACIFIC OCEAN

SOUTHERN OCEAN

0   3,000 miles
0   4,000 kilometers

This map uses different colors to show how much oil is shipped along these routes each year.

Ocean in Motion

The ocean stores huge amounts of the Sun's energy in the form of heat. Air and water currents carry that heat around the planet. All that moving heat and water affects the weather and climate—and the fish and animals that live in the ocean.

Why Map Currents?

The water of the ocean surface moves in regular patterns called surface ocean currents. Driven by tides, winds, and water temperature, currents keep the oceans in constant motion!

Mapping currents helps us navigate safely, track **pollutants**, and understand animal **migration**. For example, some marine animals and fish ride the ocean currents from place to place. Others use the currents to guide their way.

The lines on this map show the migration route of leatherback turtles and the direction of the Agulhas Current. Notice how the current influences the turtles' route.

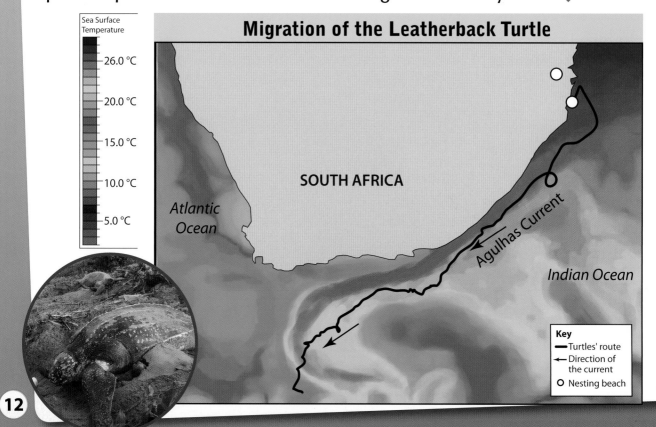

Migration of the Leatherback Turtle

Sea Surface Temperature

- 26.0 °C
- 20.0 °C
- 15.0 °C
- 10.0 °C
- 5.0 °C

Atlantic Ocean

SOUTH AFRICA

Agulhas Current

Indian Ocean

Key
- Turtles' route
- Direction of the current
- Nesting beach

How the Winds Blow

Wind is air in motion. It is caused by the uneven heating of Earth's surface. This map shows how the winds blow in different directions at different places. Winds that blow toward the equator from the northeast and the southeast are called trade winds. From about 30° to 60° north and south latitude are the westerlies. Winds near the poles are called the polar easterlies. These winds create currents at or near the ocean's surface.

Not Just Tub Toys

In 1992 thousands of plastic duck toys fell off a cargo ship in the Pacific Ocean and got caught in ocean currents. Eventually, they traveled around the globe! Scientists decided to map the ducks' journeys to help them understand currents. Look how far the ducks traveled. Some ducks didn't hit land for fifteen years!

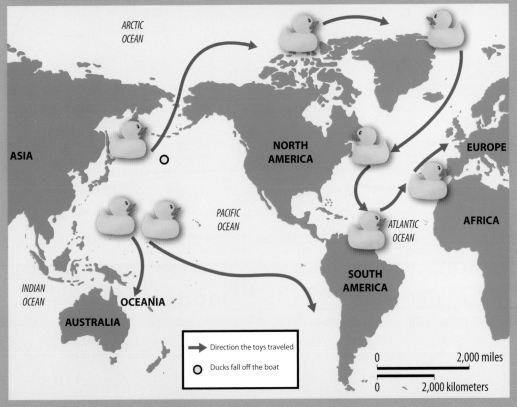

One Big Belt

Ocean water isn't the same everywhere. It's warmer in some places and cooler and saltier in others. These differences cause currents to move in a giant **global conveyor belt**. Warm water moves away from the equator and toward the poles, where the water loses heat. The cold water contracts, becoming denser and saltier, and sinks beneath the warmer water. The cold water flows back toward the equator, where it warms up again.

Did You Know?

Scientists estimate that 35 cubic feet (1 m³) of water takes one thousand years to make one trip around the global conveyor belt!

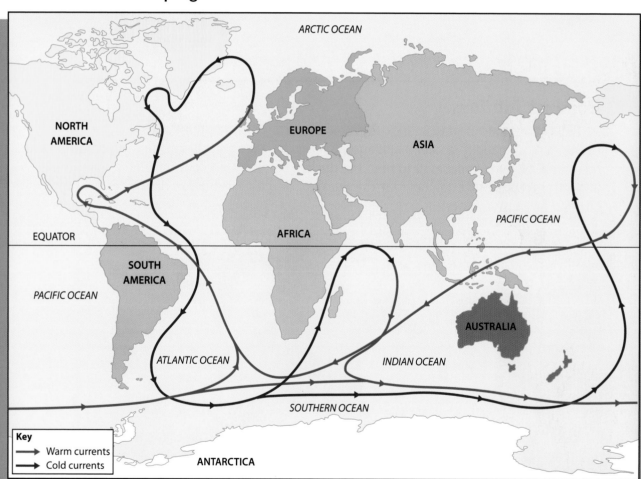

ARCTIC OCEAN

NORTH AMERICA

EUROPE

ASIA

PACIFIC OCEAN

EQUATOR

AFRICA

SOUTH AMERICA

PACIFIC OCEAN

AUSTRALIA

ATLANTIC OCEAN

INDIAN OCEAN

SOUTHERN OCEAN

Key
→ Warm currents
→ Cold currents

ANTARCTICA

Map It! Warm and Cold

The ocean's motions play a big role in shaping Earth's weather and climate. As the warm water cools, heat is released into the atmosphere.

Read It!

This map shows the movement of the ocean currents. Follow the arrows. What seems to cause the currents to change directions?

The Atlantic Ocean's Currents

The northern right whale is one of the most endangered whale species on Earth. Each spring, the whales migrate from Florida and the Caribbean north to Nova Scotia, Canada. In the fall, they reverse the route. Scientists think right whales may use currents to help them navigate during their migration. Whales also follow the currents near the Gulf of Maine because these currents bring to the surface the food and nutrients whales need.

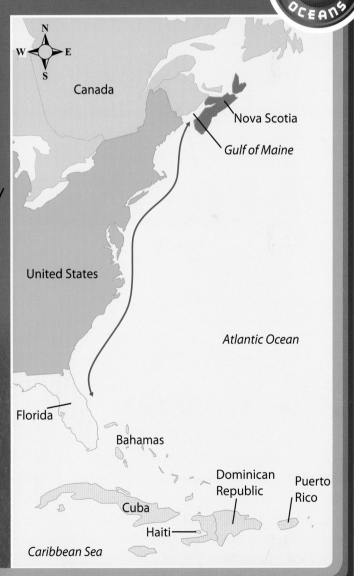

Deep, Deeper, Deepest

Scientists use modern tools to measure water depths and map the ocean floor. In the process, they uncover amazing secrets of the deep!

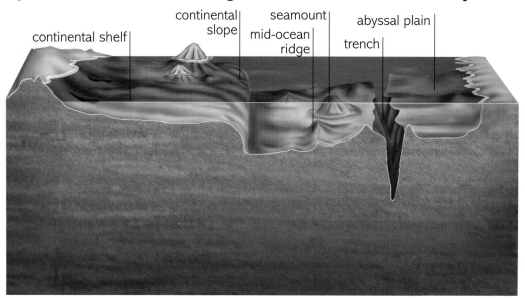

continental shelf | continental slope | seamount | mid-ocean ridge | abyssal plain | trench

This diagram shows the features of the ocean floor.

Did You Know?

Some of the tallest mountains are underwater. Many are part of underwater mountain chains called mid-ocean ridges, which can be found deep beneath the Arctic, Atlantic, Indian, and Pacific oceans. Some of the highest peaks poke through the ocean, forming islands.

World Beneath the Waves

Like the land we can see, the ocean floor is covered with plains, valleys, and mountains. This underwater landscape begins with the continental shelf, which stretches out from the edge of each continent. At the end of the shelf, the ocean floor drops off sharply. This steep slope is called the continental slope. Beyond this is a nearly flat area of the ocean floor called the abyssal plain.

In some places, deep canyons called trenches cut into the abyssal plain. Underwater **seamounts** rise above it.

The Pacific's Mariana Trench

The deepest place on Earth is the Mariana Trench in the Pacific Ocean. The bottom of the trench has openings called hydrothermal vents. The vents release hot, mineral-rich water. Bizarre creatures, such as the deep-sea anglerfish, live in the cold, dark depths of this trench where the water pressure is tremendous.

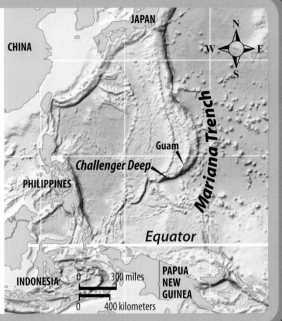

CHINA
JAPAN
PHILIPPINES
Guam
Challenger Deep
Mariana Trench
Equator
INDONESIA
PAPUA NEW GUINEA

0   300 miles
0   400 kilometers

Activity

Map the Ocean Floor!

Follow the steps to make and map your own ocean floor.

Materials
- glass or plastic aquarium
- clay or putty
- paper
- colored pencils

1. Cover the bottom of the aquarium with clay. This is your abyssal plain. Add features such as seamounts, ridges, and trenches. You can make the features different heights.

2. Sit in front of the aquarium so you are facing the long side. Look at the terrain you created. On your paper, make a rough sketch of your ocean floor. Make sure you draw and label each feature.

3. Use the colored pencils to show different heights and depths. Use yellow for the abyssal plain. Use blue for trenches. Use brown for seamounts and ridges. Keep the colors light.

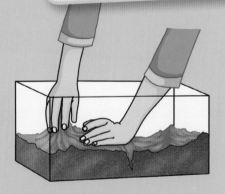

seamount
abyssal plain

4. Now use darker shades of each color to show lower points. For example, bases of seamounts would be darker brown. Deep parts of the trench would be deep blue.

Mapping the Underwater World

Scientists use tools such as **sonar** and LIDAR to map the ocean floor. They send vehicles called **submersibles** into the depths. Even space satellites high above Earth play a role in mapping the seafloor!

Did You Know?

Ocean-mapping experts help investigate airplane crashes. They create maps of the ocean floor to locate sunken aircraft.

MULTIBEAM SONAR

A multibeam sonar transmitter is attached to the bottom of a ship. It sends out several sound waves that hit the ocean floor at different angles and from different depths. The depth of an underwater feature is recorded by measuring how long it takes for the signal to be reflected back to the ship. Then that data is plotted to make a map.

SIDE-SCAN SONAR

A side-scan sonar transmitter is dragged behind a ship. It sends out sound waves and receives echoes from the ocean floor. The closer an object is to the surface, the stronger the echo. The strength of the echo creates a "picture" of the seafloor.

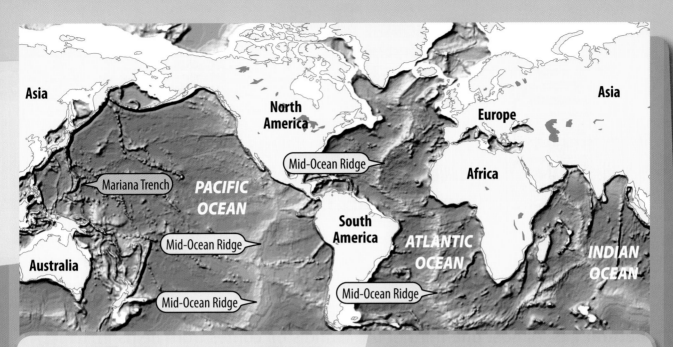

Asia

North America

Europe

Asia

Mid-Ocean Ridge

Mariana Trench

PACIFIC OCEAN

Africa

Mid-Ocean Ridge

South America

ATLANTIC OCEAN

INDIAN OCEAN

Australia

Mid-Ocean Ridge

Mid-Ocean Ridge

Mid-Ocean Ridge

Map It! The Ocean Floor

The mid-ocean ridge is an underwater mountain system that is more than 50,000 miles (80,465 km) long, making it the longest mountain range on Earth.

Read It!

Find the mid-ocean ridge on the map. Where does it appear the longest? The widest?

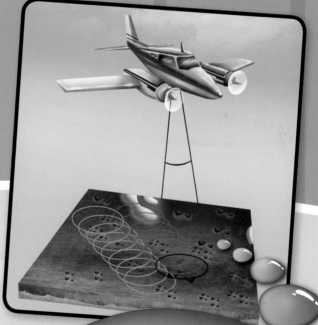

SATELLITES

Satellites orbiting Earth beam **radio waves** at the ocean. By timing how long it takes for the beams to bounce back, scientists can measure changes in the height of the sea surface.

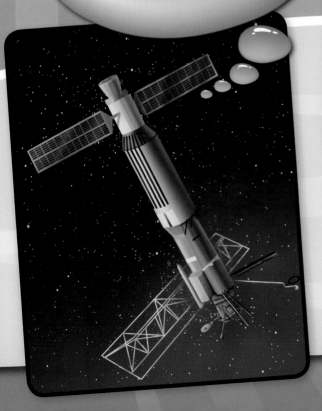

LIDAR

In a light detection and ranging, or LIDAR, system, red and green **lasers** attached to an aircraft send beams to the ocean. The red light is reflected by the water surface. The green light goes through the water and is reflected by the ocean floor. LIDAR measures the time it takes for each color laser to be reflected. The difference between the two tells scientists the depth of the ocean.

Ocean Treasures

The ocean holds all kinds of treasures, from fuel to fish. We can use maps to locate the resources we need—and even to find hidden treasures.

Underwater Wealth

The ocean supplies us with valuable resources, including oil and **natural gas**. Almost one-third of the world's oil comes from fields in the oceans. Companies use maps of the seafloor to locate **reserves** and drill for oil and natural gas near the shore. Supplies of oil and natural gas are limited. Yet people are using more and more energy each year. The oil and gas industry is moving into deeper waters in search of new reserves.

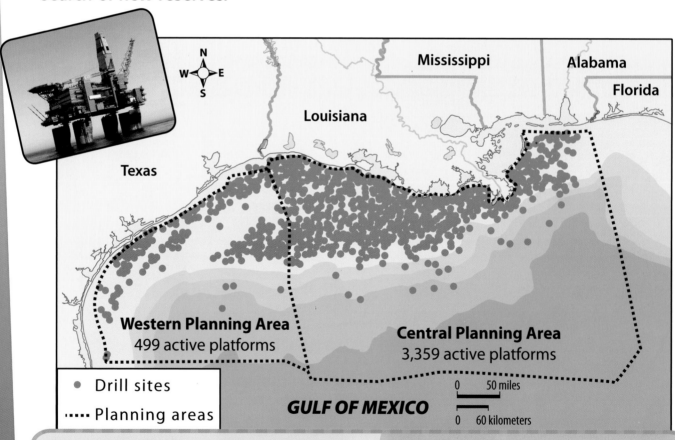

N
W — E
S

Mississippi

Alabama

Florida

Louisiana

Texas

Western Planning Area
499 active platforms

Central Planning Area
3,359 active platforms

- Drill sites
···· Planning areas

GULF OF MEXICO

0   50 miles

0   60 kilometers

Map It! Where's the Oil?
Oil reserves lie near the shore, under the continental shelf and slope.

Read It!
The orange dots show oil and natural gas drill sites off the coast of the United States in the northern Gulf of Mexico. Along the coast of what state are most of the drill sites?

King Crab Habitats
- Red king crab
- Blue king crab
- Golden king crab

Map It!
Fishing

To catch crabs, fishers drop 700-pound (318-kg) steel traps called pots 400 feet (122 m) below the ocean's surface. They use maps to help them know where to drop the pots.

Read It!

This map shows the location of Alaskan king crab in the Bering Sea. Look at the key and study the map. Where might fishers drop pots to catch red and blue king crabs?

Sea Food

The oceans are full of living treasures, too. Millions of people fish for a living, and they need detailed maps and charts to help them navigate safely. Maps also help fishers find the best fishing areas.

Activity

Crab Fishing

Make your own map showing the location of crabs. Then use the map to drop pots and catch crabs.

Materials

- 2-quart (2-liter) pot
- sand
- 20 small bolts*
- paper
- colored pencils
- string
- about 4 cups (1 liter) of water
- 4 drops of black or blue food coloring
- 2 large magnets*

*You can get bolts and magnets at a hardware store.

1. Create an ocean floor by pouring sand into the bottom of the pot. Don't smooth out the sand.

2. Place small groups of bolts in different locations in the sand. These are the crabs.

3. Draw a map of the ocean floor, showing where the crabs are.

4. In a separate container, mix the water with the food coloring. Slowly pour the water into the pot.

5. Tie a long piece of string to each magnet. These will be your crab pots.

6. Give your map to a friend. Have your friend use your map to decide where to drop the pots.

7. Pull up the magnets to see how many crabs were caught!

Living Treasures

A coral reef is home to an amazing variety of life, including one-third of all ocean fish species. Reefs also supply food and shelter to lobsters, clams, seahorses, jellyfish, sponges, sea stars, and sea turtles—to name just a few!

Coral reefs are important to people, too. They protect coasts from **erosion** by slowing incoming waves. **Organisms**, such as sponges, and minerals from coral reefs are even used to make medicine.

What Is a Reef?

Coral polyps are tiny animals that stay fixed in one place. Each soft polyp slowly builds a hard outer skeleton, or shell, for protection. A reef is made up of thousands or even millions of coral polyp shells that have grown on top of one another.

This map shows the location of the world's coral reefs. They are mostly near the equator, between the Tropic of Cancer and the Tropic of Capricorn.

Sunken Treasures

Not all treasures came to be in the oceans naturally. Some were left behind. Over the centuries, many ships—and the valuable cargo they carried—have sunk to the ocean bottom. Modern technology lets us find, explore, and map these underwater treasures that were swallowed up by the waves long ago!

Did You Know?

Multibeam side-scan sonar is used to detect objects, such as shipwrecks, on the ocean floor.

Shipwreck!

Beginning in the 1500s, ships from Europe sailed to North America to explore the land and to trade for valuable resources. The ships returned to Europe loaded with cargo, including wood, leather, chocolate, and spices. Spanish ships also carried jewels and gold and silver coins. The ships faced many dangers: uncharted reefs, strong currents, storms, and even pirate attacks! Some vessels sank during the voyage. Today, they are underwater museums for researchers and divers.

Mapping the Future

Every ocean has been harmed in some way by human activity. Ocean plants and animals—and even humans—are at risk. We can use maps to track the damage, predict future problems, and find solutions.

Oceans at Risk

Scientists have studied the effects of human activity on the oceans. What did they find? Human activity—such as pollution and overfishing—has affected every square mile of the world's oceans.

TRASHING THE OCEAN
Factories, farms, and cities sometimes dump dangerous fertilizers and other chemicals into coastal waters. People also throw trash into the oceans, which pollutes the water. Ocean mammals, fish, and seabirds often get tangled up in plastic trash, or they mistake garbage for food.

OIL SPILLS

Tankers sometimes spill oil into the oceans. On March 24, 1989, the *Exxon Valdez* oil tanker struck a reef in Alaska's Prince William Sound. Eleven million gallons (41,639 kiloliters) of oil spilled into the ocean. This map shows how far the oil spread. By the fifty-sixth day, the oil had spread 470 miles (756 km) from the accident site. The spill affected 1,300 miles (2,092 km) of shoreline.

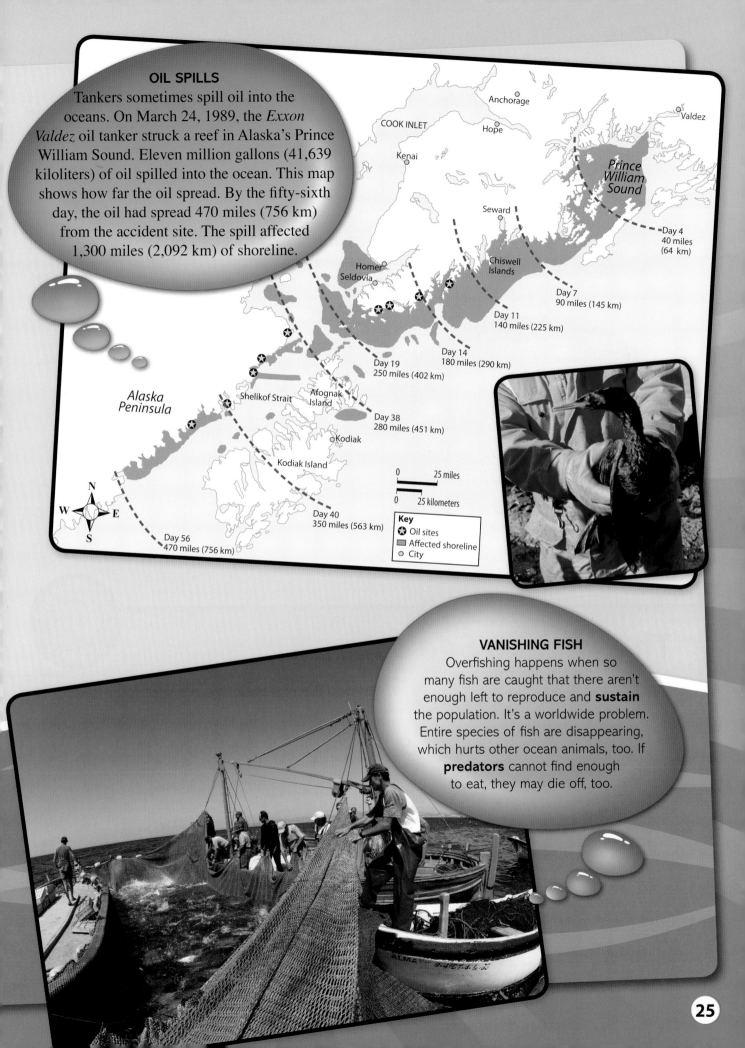

Anchorage

Valdez

COOK INLET

Hope

Kenai

Prince William Sound

Seward

Day 4
40 miles
(64 km)

Homer
Seldovia

Chiswell Islands

Day 7
90 miles (145 km)

Day 11
140 miles (225 km)

Day 14
180 miles (290 km)

Day 19
250 miles (402 km)

Alaska Peninsula

Shelikof Strait

Afognak Island

Day 38
280 miles (451 km)

Kodiak

Kodiak Island

Day 40
350 miles (563 km)

N W E S

0   25 miles
0   25 kilometers

Day 56
470 miles (756 km)

Key
* Oil sites
- Affected shoreline
○ City

VANISHING FISH

Overfishing happens when so many fish are caught that there aren't enough left to reproduce and **sustain** the population. It's a worldwide problem. Entire species of fish are disappearing, which hurts other ocean animals, too. If **predators** cannot find enough to eat, they may die off, too.

Shrinking Sea Ice

Most experts agree that pollution has changed our atmosphere and has caused the surface temperature of Earth to rise. This **global warming** has caused sea ice in the Arctic Ocean to melt. How do scientists know the Arctic ice cap is shrinking? They map Arctic sea ice and compare the ice cover from year to year.

Melting sea ice affects wildlife, such as seals and polar bears. Their home is disappearing! Melting Arctic ice will also raise ocean levels over time. Rising sea levels could cause more frequent and destructive storms and floods and cause coasts to wear away.

Arctic sea ice, 1979

Arctic sea ice, 2003

MAGNIFICENT OCEANS

The Arctic's Sea Ice

Polar bears live only near the icy Arctic waters around the North Pole. They depend on the sea ice as a platform for hunting seals, their main food. They also breed and sometimes den on the sea ice. But the sea ice is melting, which is bad news for polar bears. Scientists estimate there are between 20,000 and 25,000 polar bears in the wild. If the sea ice continues to melt, there will be fewer and fewer left.

Concerns About Coral

Arctic ice isn't the only thing at risk. So are coral reefs. Global warming has caused a rise in ocean temperatures, which has led to coral bleaching. When corals bleach, they turn white, become diseased, and may die. When corals die off, so do the plants and animals that depend on reefs for food and shelter.

Coral bleaching is bad news for us, too. We rely on reefs for many things, including food. Reefs provide a quarter of the fish we eat—enough food for about 1 billion people.

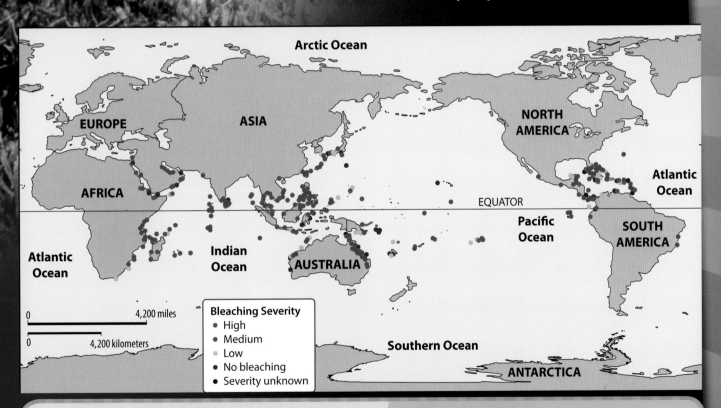

Arctic Ocean

EUROPE

ASIA

NORTH AMERICA

Atlantic Ocean

AFRICA

EQUATOR

Pacific Ocean

SOUTH AMERICA

Atlantic Ocean

Indian Ocean

AUSTRALIA

0   4,200 miles

0   4,200 kilometers

Bleaching Severity
- High
- Medium
- Low
- No bleaching
- Severity unknown

Southern Ocean

ANTARCTICA

Map It! Coral Bleaching

International, national, and conservation organizations use maps like this to identify reefs in danger and plan efforts to restore and preserve them.

Read It!

This map shows the severity of bleaching at coral reefs worldwide. Where is coral bleaching a severe problem?

Awesome Oceans

What's wonderful about our world's oceans? Read these fascinating facts and be prepared to be amazed!

- There are 25,000 islands in the Pacific Ocean. That's more than the total number of islands in the other oceans combined.

- Less than 10 percent of the ocean has been explored by humans.

- The Great Barrier Reef, the largest living structure on Earth, can be seen from space.

- The average depth of the ocean is 2.4 miles (3.9 km).

- The pressure at the deepest point in the ocean is the equivalent of fifty jumbo jets pressing down on one person.

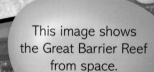

This image shows the Great Barrier Reef from space.

- Ocean life ranges in size from a single-cell microbe to the largest mammal on Earth, the blue whale.

- At least 15 percent of the ocean is covered by sea ice during part of the year.

- Ninety percent of all volcanic activity happens in the oceans.

- Some ocean pollution actually starts as air pollution, which settles into the water.

A volcanic eruption on the island of Hawaii sends lava pouring into the Pacific Ocean.

Glossary

channels Narrow waterways between landmasses.

contour lines Lines on maps connecting the points that have the same elevation.

currents Continuous movements of water in a certain direction.

endangered In danger of dying out.

erosion The process by which sand, rock, and soil are carried away by wind, water, ice, and gravity.

global conveyor belt A worldwide system of ocean currents driven by differences in the water's density and saltiness.

global warming A gradual rise in the average temperature of Earth's atmosphere and oceans.

lasers Concentrated, intense, narrow beam of light.

migration The periodic movement of animals from one place to another for feeding or breeding.

monsoons Periodic winds, especially in the Indian Ocean and in southern Asia, that bring very heavy rainfall.

natural gas Gas that comes out of Earth's crust through natural openings or drilled wells; used as a fuel.

organisms Living things, such as plants and animals.

pollutants Substances that contaminate air, soil, or water.

predators Animals that kill and eat other animals.

radar A system that determines location by measuring the time for a radio wave to an object and back to the source.

radio waves Energy that travels in the form of waves.

reserves Amounts of materials, such as oil, available for future use or need.

satellites Human-made machines that orbit Earth; used to collect information or for communication.

sea anemones Marine animals that live attached to rocks on the seafloor or on coral reefs.

seamounts Underwater mountains rising above the seafloor.

sonar A method or device for locating objects, especially underwater, by means of sound waves.

species A group of individuals having the same traits or features.

submersibles Small underwater craft used for deep-sea research.

sustain To keep alive.

tides The alternate rising and falling of the surface of the ocean that occurs twice a day; caused by the gravitational forces of the Moon and Sun on Earth.

To Learn More

Books

Burns, Loree Griffin. *Tracking Trash: Flotsam, Jetsam, and the Science of Ocean Motion*. New York: Houghton Mifflin, 2007. This is a tale of ocean trash, surface currents, and the scientists who study both. Learn how debris carried by marine currents is polluting the oceans and harming marine life.

Macquitty, Miranda. *Ocean*. DK Eyewitness Books. New York: Dorling Kindersley, 2008. Colorful photographs, detailed models of the seafloor, and informative descriptions of the undersea world and marine life combine to create an "eyewitness" view of the oceans' treasures.

McMillan, Beverly, and John A. Musick. *Oceans*. Insiders. New York: Simon & Schuster, Inc., 2007. Computer-generated art and 3-D model imagery complement the text in this title. Its fast facts, glossary, and detailed index make this a useful reference source.

Woodward, John, and Anthony Pearson. *Oceans Atlas*. New York: Dorling Kindersley, 2007. This atlas is packed with photographs and informative maps with transparent overlays, offering an in-depth look at the world's oceans.

Websites

http://floridakeys.noaa.gov/sanctuary_resources/shipwreck_trail
Dive in to explore a trail of historic shipwrecks scattered along the coral reefs and buried in the seafloor around the Florida Keys. These wrecks have fascinating tales to tell!

http://oceanservice.noaa.gov/education
At the website of the National Oceanic and Atmospheric Administration (NOAA), check out ocean-related mysteries, tutorials, case studies, games, activities, and many other resources.

www.pbs.org/wgbh/nova/abyss
This PBS website follows a research expedition to study the unusual seafloor features known as "black smokers" at an undersea ridge off the coast of Washington State. Learn about the bizarre creatures that make their home in this harsh environment.

www.epa.gov/OWOW/oceans/coral
Learn all about coral reefs, why they are important, and what you can do to protect the oceans, the coasts, and especially this unique habitat.

Index

abyssal plain, 16, 17
Agulhas Current, 12
Alaskan king crab, 21
Antarctica, 9
Arctic Ocean, 9, 16, 26
Arctic sea ice (Arctic Ice Cap), 26, 27
Asia, 9
Atlantic Ocean, 7, 8, 9, 15, 16
Australia, 8, 9

bathymetric maps, 7
Bering Sea, 21
blue whale, 29

Challenger Deep, 8
channels, 9
climate, 5, 12, 14
coast, 7, 15, 20, 22, 26
coastal waters, 24
compass rose, 6
continental shelf, 16, 20
continental slope, 16, 20
contour lines, 10
coral bleaching, 27
coral polyps, 22
coral reef, 5, 22, 27

deep-sea anglerfish, 17

equator, 6, 13, 14
erosion, 22
Exxon Valdez oil tanker, 25

fishing, 6, 10, 21

global conveyor belt, 14
global warming, 26, 27
Great Barrier Reef, 8, 28
Gulf of Maine, 15
Gulf of Mexico, 20
Gulf Stream, 15

habitat, 5
Hawaii, 29
hydrothermal vents, 17

Indian Ocean, 7, 9, 16
International Hydrographic Organization, 7

key, 6, 7, 10, 21

lasers, 19
latitude, 6, 17, 13
leatherback turtle, 12
light detection and ranging (LIDAR), 18, 19
longitude, 6

map scale, 6
Mariana Trench, 8, 17
meridians, 6
mid-ocean ridge, 16, 19
migration, 12, 15
monsoons, 9
multibeam sonar, 18, 23

natural gas, 20
nautical charts, 7, 10, 11
North Pole, 6, 26
northern right whale, 15

ocean (water) currents, 7, 10, 12, 13, 14, 15
ocean floor, 16, 17, 18, 19, 23
oil, 11, 20, 25
oil spills, 25
organisms, 22
overfishing, 24, 25

Pacific Ocean, 7, 8, 9, 13, 16, 17, 28, 29
polar bears, 26
polar easterlies, 13

poles (North and South), 6, 13, 14
pollutants, 12
pollution, 24, 26, 29
predators, 25
prime meridian, 6
Prince William Sound, 25

radar, 7
radio waves, 19
reserves, 20

satellites, 7, 18, 19
sea anemones, 5
seamount, 16, 17
shipwreck, 11, 23
side-scan sonar, 18, 23
sonar, 18
South Pole, 6
Southern (Antarctic) Ocean, 7, 9
submersibles, 18
Sun's energy, 12
surface ocean currents, 12

thematic maps, 7
tides, 6, 10, 12
topographic maps, 7
trade, 8, 11, 22
trade winds, 13
travel (transportation), 5, 7, 8, 10
trench, 8, 16, 17
Tropic of Cancer, 22
Tropic of Capricorn, 22

weather, 5, 12, 14
westerlies, 13
winds, 12, 13, 15